WHAT HAVE WE DONE

A. Carpenter

WHAT HAVE WE DONE

AN IN-DEPTH STUDY OF THE ACCOMPLISHMENTS OF THE BIDEN ADMINISTRATION

gatekeeper press™

Tampa, Florida

What Have We Done: An In-Depth Study of the Accomplishments of the Biden Administration

Published by Gatekeeper Press
7853 Gunn Hwy., Suite 209
Tampa, FL 33626
www.GatekeeperPress.com

ISBN (paperback): 9781662951473

Contents

Foreword
(By The Author)

DURING THIS PIVOTAL ELECTION YEAR IN WHICH AN INCUMBENT ADMINISTRATION IS SEEKING RE-ELECTION, AN IN-DEPTH STUDY OF THE ACCOMPLISHMENTS OF THE CURRENT PRESIDENCY AND HOW THEIR PERSONAL LEADERSHIP AND ADMINISTRATION HAVE BENEFITED THE NATION—AND THE WORLD AS A WHOLE—IS BOTH TIMELY AND PROPER.

Preamble to the United States Constitution

We the People of the United States, in Order to form a more perfect Union, establish Justice, insure domestic Tranquility, provide for the common defense, promote the general Welfare, and secure the Blessings of Liberty to ourselves and our Posterity, do ordain and establish this Constitution for the United States of America.

Article II, Section 1 of the Constitution

The executive Power shall be vested in a President of the United States of America. He shall hold his Office during the Term of four Years, and, together with the Vice President, chosen for the same Term, be elected.

THE PREAMBLE SPECIFIES SIX PURPOSES FOR WHICH THE CONSTITUTION WAS FORMED. THIS BOOK PRESENTS A COMPREHENSIVE AND DETAILED ACCOUNTING OF THE ACCOMPLISHMENTS OF THIS ADMINISTRATION IN EACH OF THOSE PURPOSES. THESE ARE BROKEN DOWN INTO SEVERAL VITAL AREAS OF FOCUS AND PROVIDE A LOOK AT THE ACHIEVEMENTS OF THE CURRENT PRESIDENCY IN EACH OF THOSE CRITICAL AREAS.

It is the hope of this author that each reader may find within the pages of this book, valuable information that may assist them in making the best decisions, as each of them weighs their personal, critical vote in this important election year.

A. Carpenter

CHAPTER 1

"To Form a More Perfect Union"

What are some of the most critical elements of continuing to establish and "To Form a More Perfect Union." that strengthen and promote harmony and longevity in our union?

- A Federal Executive Administration that works well with the Congress and the states to establish policies that provide a clear delineation of the rights and responsibilities of the Federal Government, from those of the States, as outlined in the constitution. That Administration, and the States, should foster a cooperative relationship with each other, and maintain a healthy balance of both their sovereignty and interdependence, as outlined in the constitution. They should work together for what is in the simplest terms, "The security of life, liberty and the pursuit of happiness," of each individual citizen of this great nation.

- An Executive Administration is the representative of our union with all other nations; it should be one that protects first and foremost the sovereignty and security of the United States, while at the same time acts to assure that we are good neighbors.
- An Administration that conducts healthy trade relations with other nations that are bilaterally fair and equitable, while protecting our own national health first.

The following pages of this Chapter list the ways in which this Administration has been able preserve and strengthen "A more perfect Union."

5

12

"To Form a More Perfect Union"

"To Form a More Perfect Union"

"To Form a More Perfect Union"

CHAPTER **2**

"Establish Justice"

What are some of the most critical elements of forming and continuing to "Establish Justice" for each individual person, our communities, states, and the nation as a whole?

- An Executive who in their personal life demonstrates a deep reverence for the law, and then expands that reverence by establishing an Administration that exemplifies that same devotion and respect for the law.
- A Presidency, Administration, and Executive Branch that first and foremost honors the Constitution as the Supreme Law of the Land and seeks to follow it as the first principle of Governance with Justice.
- An Executive Administration whose Department of Justice has a deep commitment to the law and administers the law with resolution, evenly, and

without prejudice or bias with regards to race, religion, political affiliation, economic status, or any other personal condition, but acts solely on the basis of each person's obedience to the law.

- An Executive Administration that is firm in law enforcement, while at the same time is diligent in being as sure as possible of the innocence or guilt of the accused. Then once a person is convicted, that they are properly subject to the requirements of the law without favoritism or bias. The Administration should seek justice in a way that promotes a rehabilitation and growth toward each offender becoming, if possible, a beneficial member of society.

The following pages of this Chapter list the ways in which the Biden Administration has been able preserve, strengthen, and "Establish Justice."

What Have We Done

29

"Establish Justice"

"Establish Justice"

34

35

37

"Establish Justice"

42

"Establish Justice"

CHAPTER 3

"Insure Domestic Tranquility"

First, let us define Domestic Tranquility. A simple definition is, "Peace and Calm" in our lives and homes. It means that all persons can walk down the sidewalk in their neighborhoods and cities and be safe from harm or theft, and that there is law and order in our communities. That we can tuck our children into bed at night and they will be safe there. It means that there is peace between persons, cities, and states. It also means that as individual citizens and a nation, we feel safe with regard to any threat from other countries or their agents.

What are some of the most critical elements of forming and continuing to "Insure Domestic Tranquility" for each individual person, our communities, states, and the nation as a whole?

- One of the first principles that ensures domestic tranquility is each individual's respect for the rights, safety, happiness, and dignity of every other person with whom they interact, so long as that other person practices the same respect for others. An Executive who in their personal life demonstrates this respect, and then expands that by establishing an Administration that exemplifies that same respect, and insures it to all well-acting members of our great nation.

- An Administration that promotes well-trained police forces and court systems throughout the nation. One that respects and cherishes the individual, while at the same time demonstrates that respect by speedily providing equal protection to all law-abiding members of our society without preference, prejudice, or bias.

- An Administration that promotes a controlled and equitable policy for the execution of the laws established by congress for the security of our borders and intelligent immigration. This security would seek as much as possible to insure that persons entering our country will be beneficial members of society, who will contribute to our betterment and not be likely to perpetrate crimes, or be a burden on our existing citizenry. They will promote a balance of compassion for those seeking a better life, and the continued quality of life for those already here. To establish an orderly, secure, and fair Administration of the immigration process, in keeping with the established laws.

- An Executive Administration whose policies prize and promote the safety and well-being of all law-abiding citizens, allowing them to have safety in their persons, homes, communities, and the nation at large. In this great land of free enterprise, any person who in an integrate manner applies their intellect, talent, and hard work, can advance themselves. They can safely accumulate property, i.e. clothing, a place to live, land, conveyance, a business, equipment, tools, and all manner of property. All persons should be tranquil in the lawful, respectful use and enjoyment of their property, no matter what level of ownership they may have. We each respect the ownership of others, while at the same time we can apply our industry to expand our own ownership. My mother taught her children a simple little rule. She said, "Before you take something, answer this one question: Is it yours?"

- An Executive Administration whose policies promote honest, respectful, and open debate of all political views and affiliations, where all persons are free to express their opinions and are not subject to any bias because of their personal beliefs, so long as those beliefs respect the law, and each person is reciprocally respectful of all others.

- An Executive Administration whose policies balance the promotion of free enterprise while at the same time requiring fairness and equity when pursuing economic goals.

The following pages of this Chapter list the ways in which the Biden Administration has been able to preserve, strengthen, and "Insure Domestic Tranquility."

49

What Have We Done

51

53

56

58

59

61

65

"Provide for the Common Defense"

What are some of the most critical elements to "Provide for the Common Defense" of each individual person, our communities, states, and the nation as a whole?

- An Executive who in their personal life demonstrates a deep reverence for the rights enumerated within our Constitution and the Bill of Rights, and then expands that reverence by establishing an Administration that exemplifies that same respect for those rights, and vigorously defends them.
- A Presidency, Administration, and Executive Branch that promotes a strong national military, one that is used first of all for the defense of the rights of American Citizens, and then second for the world at large; but that does so with wisdom and respect for the sovereignty and culture of all nations that seek to advance their own people in a way that promotes opportunity and freedom for the world as a whole.

- An Executive Administration that expands the safety of the citizens of our nation to the world at large, and does all that is possible to ensure their safety while in other countries. For many years, it was a sacred fundamental doctrine of the US Government to protect our citizens all over the world. The world knew that if they detained or injured a U.S. citizen without due process or just cause, that they brought the entire might of this country down upon their head. Every effort was made diplomatically, and, if needed, militarily to secure the safety of each citizen, regardless of their station, and return them home to their loved ones. This of course was based on each person's responsibility to conduct themselves in a respectful and courteous manner while visiting another country and to respect the laws of that land.

- An Executive Administration whose international actions and diplomatic policies use the strength of our nation to promote peace and freedom in the world at large. They seek peaceful solutions to conflicts, with fairness and respect, while putting first priority on our own best interests and security.

- An Executive Administration that promotes defenses from all types of dangers to our citizens. This includes defenses against harmful drugs being distributed to our population, against diseases, unfair trade conditions, invasions, terrorist acts, or acts of violence, especially mass violence against our citizenry from other countries or radical factions within our own society.

The following pages of this Chapter list the ways in which the Biden Administration has been able to strengthen and "Provide for the Common Defense."

77

78

83

86

89

CHAPTER **5**

"Promote the General Welfare"

What are some of the most critical elements of "Promoting the General Welfare" for each individual person, our communities, states, and the nation as a whole?

- A Presidency, Administration, and Executive Branch that promotes general welfare, establishes a government that promotes an environment where all its citizens are as free as possible to develop their skills and talents, and then to apply those in a free and open market through business and employment. They do this in such a way as to maximize each person's ability to provide services and goods to others, and enables them to receive the greatest compensation possible in exchange for those goods and services. Such an environment will strive to keep the process of establishing and operating enterprises as open and uncomplicated as possible, while at the same time creating the proper controls that will protect the safety and security of the general citizenry of our own nation and the world at large.

- An Administration and Executive Branch that provides these protections will promote the welfare of each citizen's physical body. This is done by working to ensure that products and services are safe for use and consumption, and will promote the physical well-being of each person, but does so in a way that is not so cumbersome that the process of organizing and operating businesses stifles or discourages enterprises.

- An Executive Administration that promotes the general welfare will work to help establish policies, programs, and institutions that promote the general educational and emotional welfare of each individual, without prejudice or bias, and without regard to their race, religion, political affiliation, or economic condition. These measures would be specifically designed for the development of children in an environment of security, safety, and love. This would also extend to the educational opportunities and development of adolescents, young, and older adults.

- An Executive Administration that promotes the general welfare would work with the Congress to help establish laws and a system of Justice that safeguards each person in the use and enjoyment of the property and resources that they have been able to accumulate through their enterprise and industry. At the same time, allowing all persons equal opportunity to similarly advance and be secure in the enjoyment of the fruits of their industry and enterprise.

- An Executive Administration that promotes the general welfare would work to assist those in need in a way that, while helping, still protects the general welfare of each person by promoting the happiness and dignity of work, self-reliance, and contributing to the society in which we live. It is difficult to be happy when we are living off of the labor of others, and not doing all that we can to provide for ourselves and contribute to the world around us. Likewise, it is difficult to be happy when the resources we obtain through our own industry and enterprise are diminished because they are given to those who are able to provide for their own needs, but are in a system that promotes or perpetuates a lifestyle that lives off the sweat of another person's brows. Assistance that promotes the general welfare blesses the individual while they may be in need, and aids them in a timely return to self-reliance, but also assists the public at large by not placing an undue burden on them to provide assistance to those who are able, thus diminishing their ability to provide for their own needs.

- An Executive Administration that promotes the general welfare would work to establish a system of good health care in a way that is affordable and available in a timely manner to all persons, while at the same time balancing the rights of each person with their responsibility to be as self-reliant as possible.

- An Executive Administration that promotes the general welfare would provide proper security and protection of intellectual enterprise by operating agencies for patents and copyrights as per the laws established by the Congress.

The following pages of this Chapter list the ways in which the Biden Administration has been able to preserve and "Promote the General Welfare."

"Promote the General Welfare"

CHAPTER 6

"Secure the Blessing of Liberty to Ourselves and Our Posterity"

What are some of the most critical elements that will continue to "Secure the Blessings of Liberty to Ourselves and Our Posterity" for our communities, states, and the nation as a whole?

- A Presidency, Administration, and Executive Branch that first and foremost reveres our history and the struggle that gave birth to and preserved our liberty, the Constitution, our free enterprise, due process under the law, and as Lincoln said, "Cherishes Liberty as the heritage of all persons, in all lands, everywhere." This reverence and cherishing of Liberty will lead to great efforts to secure its blessings for ourselves and our posterity.

- An Executive Administration with a deep love of Liberty will pursue fiscal responsibility that seeks to minimize the financial burden of government, which must be borne by the citizens in the form of taxes. Every building, employee, service, facility, instrument, and tool provided by the government has to be paid for. Careful evaluation of cost versus benefit must be made before each expenditure. Resources need to be maximized. We must seek to balance our spending with our income. To burden ourselves and future generations with unnecessary debt is to erode the foundations of Liberty. How can we or our posterity be free if we are yoked with a huge burden of debt?

- An Executive Administration that is open and transparent in their conducting of the government, answering to the governed from whom they derive the power and authority to execute the governance of the people. An Administration that protects free speech and the freedom of the press without interfering or seeking to influence the instruments of these freedoms. This requires an Administration that is willing to be criticized and censured by the people and the press, and that is committed to conducting their business in the open air and daylight. Only this kind of transparency can preserve Liberty.

- An Administration that secures the blessing of Liberty to ourselves and our posterity by working to secure and facilitate each citizen exercising their right to vote according to the dictates of their own conscience. This is accomplished by making the process of voting open and easily accessible to all persons who are citizens of our country, and as such are eligible to vote, while at the same time protecting against illegal voting by those who are not citizens and who do not have a legal right to vote. A household cannot allow its governance to be influenced or controlled by those who are not members of that household. The law is clear and must be respected, that only citizens of this nation may vote in its elections. It must be equally clear that all citizens must have a simple and easy process to verify their eligibility, register, and to exercise their vote.

- An Executive Administration that will secure the blessings of Liberty to ourselves and our posterity by promoting and following the democratic doctrine of "the rule of the majority." Because the members of a diverse and free society will nearly always see each issue from many points of view, and because every intelligent, honest, and sincere person will most always have some valid viewpoint on an issue, and because that view point may vary from that of another's, open and respectful discussion and debate of all these issues is critical to a country establishing a system of governance and laws that allow the greatest freedoms possible, while protecting the rights of each individual, and protecting the safety and security of the society as a whole. Once we have freely and respectfully debated a question, and the process of give-and-take compromise has produced a law, and that law has been voted on and accepted by the majority; then to preserve order, tranquility, and Liberty, all persons must then commit to obeying the law. This process may go through several iterations over time, and we must have faith that with time and experience, the opinions of the majority will move toward an ultimate justice and truth.

- An Executive Administration that will greatly advance the security of liberty to ourselves and our posterity by working to treat all people of all walks of life with an equality under the law and by promoting procedures and policies of governance, education, and Administration that facilitates the attitudes and actions of the people as a whole, to view each person as an individual, valued and judged, as Martin Luther King Jr. said, "not by the color of their skin but by the content of their character," nor by their religion, personal culture, or political affiliations.

The following pages of this Chapter list the ways in which the Biden Administration has preserved, strengthened, and "Secured the Blessings of Liberty to Ourselves and Our Posterity."

125

"Secure the Blessing of Liberty to Ourselves and Our Posterity"

135

137

Notes

Notes

151

Post Script

It will be clear to the reader that the author of this book does not believe that the Current Administration has performed well during the time that they have been in office. What I hope is equally clear, is that my lists of the accomplishments of the Current Administration (or the lack thereof) are a spoof. Of course, this Administration has done *some* good. In my opinion, they have also done significant harm. In simple terms, asking the question, "After three plus years of their being in office, is America and the world better?" My truthful and sincere answer would have to be "No."

I would invite each reader to reflect and give their own answer to some of the following questions:

- Is our country and the world more secure and safe? Does each person and family feel more secure and safe in their persons, home, and community?
- Has the Executive Administration of our border and immigration procedures been administered in an intelligent and thoughtful manner that has produced

order and security, and improved the quality of life for the citizens of our country?

- Is our economy stronger and more stable? Is each individual person and family better off financially?
- Does each of us feel more united as Americans? Do we feel more pride in our country? Do we feel our lives and those of our children and grandchildren are on solid ground, that they are safe and secure, that the future is bright?

I hope that what is also evident in this book is that I love our country and believe in its goodness. I believe in Liberty and that the security and tranquility of each person should be the object of government. I believe that freedom and free enterprise are the right of every person, and that true government is of the people, by the people, and for the people. A government derives its just powers from the consent of the governed. That true government should be organized by the people to secure life, liberty, and the pursuit of happiness for all its people, and to do so equally, without bias or prejudice, based **only** on the content of each person's character.

I believe that it is the responsibility of each elected or appointed agent of the government to serve the best interests of the individual citizen and the country as a whole. This should be the root basis for each action of each agent of the government, and not the party line. Each agent of the government, whether elected, hired, or appointed should serve with integrity. They should conduct their business with an open mind and seek the truth by having respectful exchanges with all points of view, sincerely evaluate, and work for the best, common good of all.

I believe that each of us has a fundamental responsibility to do good and contribute to the society in which we live in a positive, meaningful way. This can be in our family, neighborhood, community, state, and nation. Each act of service, each act of good, large or small, contributes to the benefit of the whole. Each of us has a responsibility to do all that we can to be self-reliant and help others to do the same. Each of us needs to treat those around us with respect, courtesy, and kindness. Each of us needs to do our part to make our communities safe, to respect and protect the lives, happiness, and property of others, as well as our own. Again, I repeat what my mother taught her children, "Before you take something, answer this one question: is it yours?"

As anyone who reads this book can tell, I am a simple man. I do not hold any advanced degrees in education; I have no great works to my credit, or fame, or wealth.

I am a tradesman, a worker with my hands. Many will say that the thoughts expressed on these pages are not realistic, that I do not understand human nature, that they are a wonderful dream, but are the product of too simple a mind. I would paraphrase Kennedy and answer: "Some men see things as they are and ask why? I see things as they should be and ask why not?" Is it not best to have an image of things "as they should be" and constantly use that standard as a measure of what we are doing now to arrive at that station?

I would ask each reader to carefully consider your vote. Evaluate and choose wisely. I believe a great deal depends on this. Review the questions presented in each Chapter of this book and add your own. Evaluate—who will be the best chief executive of our nation? Who will be most able to establish an Executive Administration that will lead our country in a good direction? Listen to other's points of view and thoughts, consider them, then make your best decision, AND VOTE.

Best Wishes,
A. Carpenter